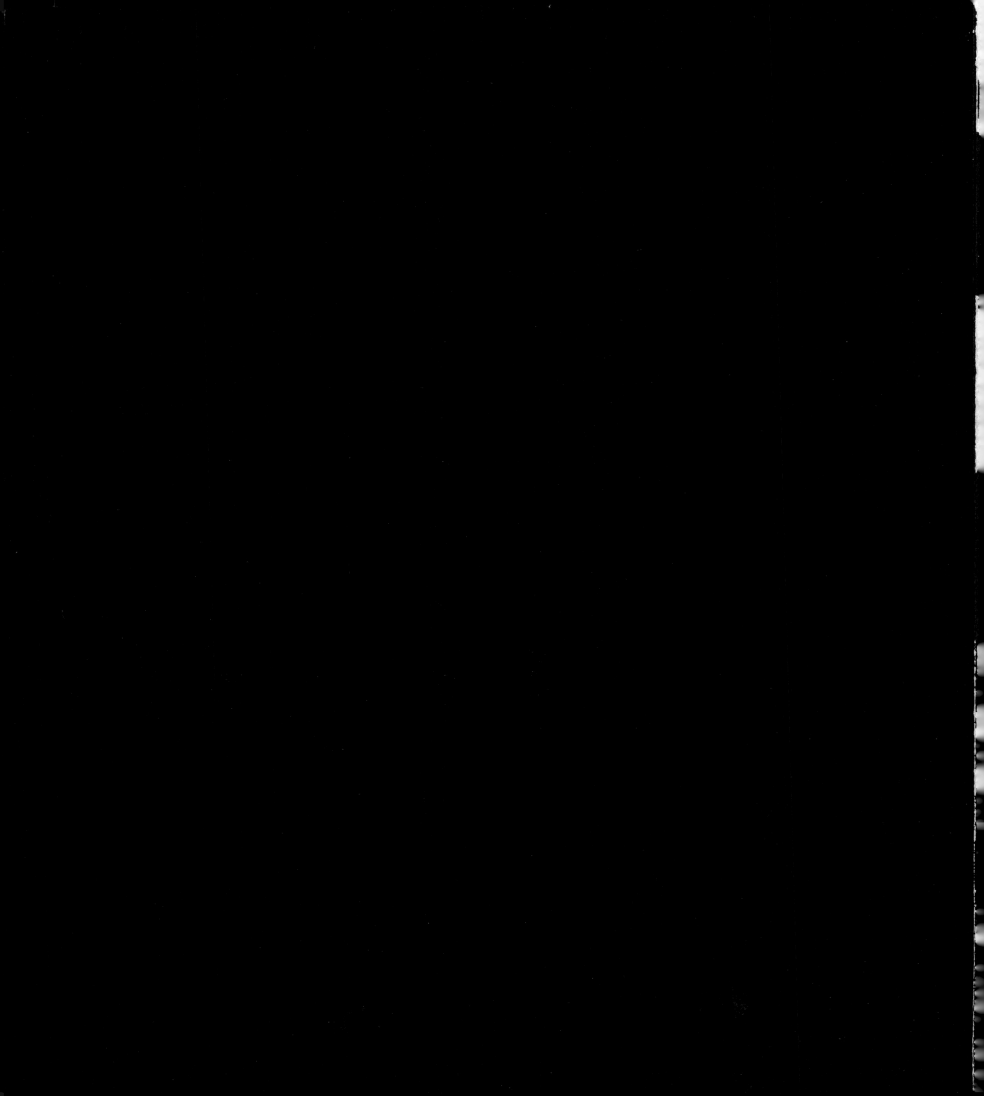

LAND OF LIGHT

Snerruútgáfan ehf.

LAND OF LIGHT

PHOTOGRAPHS BY HAUKUR SNORRASON

Foreword
Ólafur Ragnar Grímsson
President of Iceland

◆

Texts
Magnús Tumi Guðmundsson
geophysicist

Bessastaðir – Residence of the President of Iceland.

Foreword by
Ólafur Ragnar Grímsson
President of Iceland

The ever-living play of light; the glory of creation in striking contrasts; the symphony of colours. Can a country ever be imagined which combines all this?

Blue mountains and white glaciers, green plains and black barren sands; extinct craters and rough lava blanketed with soft moss; beautifully coloured flowers on rough gravelbanks. The murmuring of a brook in its verdant enclave between mountains, the distant song of birds, the eerie silence of the wilderness. Nature's spectrum, the inspiration for our poets' and painters' immortal art.

Lofty cliffs and deep gullies, the land's heart beating in hot springs and billowing white clouds of steam, the lava seething when hoarse primeval forces growl through volcanoes or give birth to new islands in the sea, the awesome force of glaciers that burst out of their icy fetters: all these are a testimony to the fact that the creation of the world is still going on in Iceland, that the Almighty is still busily at work.

Dawn breaking on the moors, sunset at the sea's horizon, bright spring nights, the northern lights sporting through the heavens in the winter darkness, the ever-changing light of each new day, each new moment.

The mountain that once was blue turns brown with a green sheen upon it, then is suddenly wreathed in a red glow, then perhaps black or golden or grey, or hidden in a white haze.

Icelandic nature is a fantastic world, a banquet of light and colour, the home of beauty. It is our great fortune to be sitting in the centre of the stage and be able to share these glories with you.

The Lakagígar crater series, formed in 1783 when the largest flood of lava known on Earth in historical times flowed from them.
The lava flow covered almost 600 km² and toxic gases produced by the eruption wrought serious damage upon vegetation and livestock.
Much of Iceland's livestock died from the effects, and famine followed.

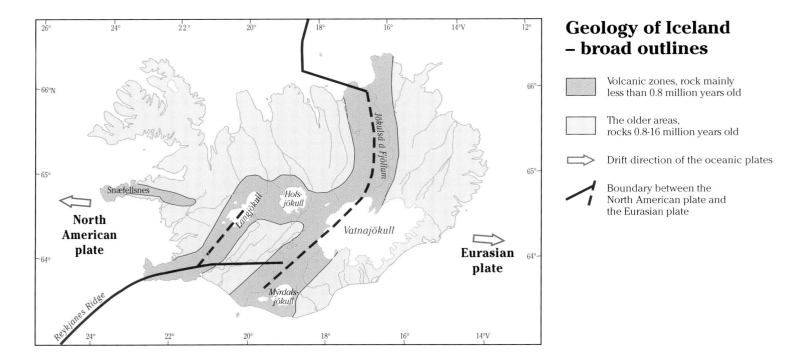

Geology of Iceland
– broad outlines

Volcanic zones, rock mainly
less than 0.8 million years old

The older areas,
rocks 0.8-16 million years old

Drift direction of the oceanic plates

Boundary between the
North American plate and
the Eurasian plate

Iceland's geographical position and geological conditions make it completely different from most other countries. Its nature is unusual, with volcanoes, glaciers, geothermal springs, sands, wilderness, bird cliffs and grassy plains, but few woods. The weather is changeable and some visitors even complain of sleeplessness during the bright summer nights, however much the Icelanders themselves may cherish them. Over the 1,100 years since their country was first settled by Vikings, the Icelanders have fought a battle for survival against the forces of nature, often facing incredible odds. It is fair to say that only with the technological advances of the 20th century did the Icelanders manage to utilize their natural resources on land and at sea for their own benefit on any significant scale.

Geologically speaking, Iceland is a young country. The oldest rocks that have been found are 14-16 million years old, on the outermost promontories of the West Fjords and East Fjords. By comparison, rocks can be found in West Greenland which are almost 4,000 million years old. The timescale is sometimes illustrated by comparing the age of the Earth with a single day: the oldest rock found in Iceland would have been formed only five minutes ago. Iceland's existence in the mid-Atlantic needs to be understood in the context of volcanism and plate tectonics on Earth. The outermost layer of the Earth's crust is the lithosphere, brittle and cold. Beneath it is the astenosphere, where the mantle rock is warmer and more viscous. The lithosphere is divided into plates that drift across the astenosphere. Ridges are common on the ocean floor, marking the boundary where two astenospheric plates are spreading apart from each other. One such ridge, the Mid-Atlantic Ridge, stretches right along the floor of the Atlantic Ocean, but in Iceland it rises above the surface of the sea, which is highly unusual. The explanation for this, and therefore for Iceland's very existence, is found in the depths of the Earth. Iceland is what is known as a hot spot, a place of exceptional volcanic activity. Hot spots are thought to be the product of localized upwelling of hot matter from deep within the Earth's mantle, known as mantle plumes. Iceland's unique combination of a hot spot and mid-ocean ridge explains the evolution and character of its volcanic activity. The western part of the country belongs to the North American plate and is moving westwards at 1 cm

per year. The eastern part belongs to the Eurasian plate and is moving eastwards at the same rate. The volcanic zone running through Iceland from Reykjanes in the southwest to Öxarfjörður in the northeast marks the plate boundary.

A wider range of magma is produced by volcanic eruptions in Iceland than on oceanic ridges, due to the interaction of the mantle plume and the oceanic ridge. Iceland's northerly location makes it one of the few places on Earth where subglacial volcanic eruptions occur. Subglacial eruptions during the Ice Age produced hyaloclastite mountains of various shapes, which characterize volcanic zones in Iceland.

For at least two million years, Iceland's surface was repeatedly covered by Ice Age glaciers. The older parts of the country came into being before the Ice Age began, and have fairly regular-shaped lava strata. Their characteristic features are deep valleys and fjords which have been carved out by Ice Age glaciers. In the volcanic zones, on the other hand, steep ridges and table mountains were formed by eruptions beneath the glaciers. Instead of spreading out in the form of lava, the pyroclastic materials piled up into cones which melted their way through the ice. During warmer interglacial periods, the glacial cover retreated from the land, allowing lava to flow freely and form the plains between the hyaloclastite mountains. In this way, the landscape of the volcanic zones took shape.

The forces which shaped Iceland during the Ice Age are still at work. Beneath Vatnajökull and Mýrdalsjökull glaciers are active volcanoes which have erupted on numerous occasions in historical times. Some have caused massive glacier outburst floods, for example during the eruption in the Gjálp volcano in the western part of Vatnajökull in autumn 1996. Outburst floods from Mýrdalsjökull are generally even more dramatic. Glacier outburst floods have played a major part in creating the extensive sandflats of southeast Iceland. The magnificent canyon now forming the course of the river Jökulsá á Fjöllum was created several thousand years ago in a truly catastrophic outburst flood which was many times more powerful than the 1996 one – even though this swamped an area of almost 1,000 km^2 on the Skeiðarársandur outwash sands.

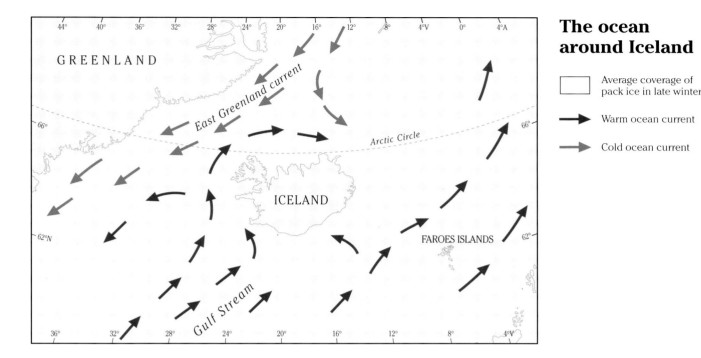

The ocean around Iceland

	Average coverage of pack ice in late winter
➡	Warm ocean current
➡	Cold ocean current

The confluence of the Gulf Stream, which flows along the eastern coast of North America and past Iceland all the way north to the Barents Sea, and cold polar currents, lies just north of Iceland This means that the boundary between or polar climate and temperate climate lies just north of Iceland at present. As a result, Iceland is in the path of fronts which bring precipitation and changeable weather. Thanks to the Gulf Stream, the climate in Iceland is much warmer than is normally the case at such a northerly latitude. At the confluence of warm and cold seas, moreover, are the bounteous fishing grounds which have been the mainstay of Iceland's economy throughout the 20th century.

Ever since Iceland was settled eleven hundred years ago, its climate has been prone to change. For most of the settlement period in the ninth and tenth centuries the climate was favourable and the glaciers covered a smaller area than at present. In the late Middle Ages the climate cooled and the glaciers began advancing. From around 1600 until the end of the 19th century, a cold period reigned in Iceland, known as the Little Ice Age. At that time sea ice commonly blocked the coasts of north Iceland in late winter. An example of the advance of the glaciers is known from historical records, when Breiðamerkurjökull descended upon the farm at Breiðá in southeast Iceland. The glacier was apparently no threat to the same farm when Njál's Saga was written in the 13th century, since the hero Kári Sölmundarson moved there in great honour after his reconciliation with his one-time arch-enemy Flosi, instigator of the burning of Njál's farm, a turning-point in this famous Saga. The former site of Breiðá is thought to be no longer underneath the glacier, as glaciers have been retreating this century in pace with the warming climate.

Until very recently the Icelandic nation depended for its livelihood on the whims of the forces of nature. If the cold weather persisted and sea ice blocked the coasts of the north and the east, people suffered hardship and even died from famine. Ever since Iceland was settled, volcanic eruptions have intermittently disrupted people's livelihoods. The greatest disaster of this kind was the "Skaftá fires" (Skaftáreldar) of 1783-84, which produced the largest lava flow known in historical times anywhere on Earth. Another side-effect was the volcanic gases which entered the atmosphere, enveloping Iceland and causing significant cooling in the entire northern hemisphere for a year or two. The majority of livestock in Iceland died then, and so did one-fifth of the population from the subsequent famine. It was even suggested that Iceland was in fact uninhabitable and its whole population ought to be shipped off to Jutland in Denmark, but fortunately the idea was never put into practice.

There is a good case for arguing that Iceland lay on the border of the habitable world for centuries, at least in medieval European terms. Written sources, archaeological findings and changes in vegetation show that Iceland was settled about 1,100 years ago. Greenland was settled by people from Iceland about 100 years later. When the climate cooled in the 14th and 15th centuries, the Nordic settlements in Greenland disappeared; historical records remain mysteriously silent about their fate. In Iceland, man's cohabitation with nature was a troublesome relationship: felling of trees and grazing by sheep joined forces with the Little Ice Age and volcanic eruptions to destroy the highland vegetation. Today, only just over 1% of the surface of Iceland is covered by woodland, compared with an estimated quarter at the beginning of the settlement. At the same time, large areas of land have been eroded and the soil cover has been lost.

Iceland's position has changed enormously in the course of a century. Around 1900 the industrial revolution was ushered in with the introduction of trawlers. A huge intensification of the fishing effort with motorized vessels transformed Iceland from one of the poorest nations in Europe at the turn of the century, to one of the richest fifty years later. But for as long as the Icelanders continue to base their livelihoods above all on the sea, climate changes can have crucial consequences. Research suggests that the greenhouse effect and global warming could produce radical changes in ocean currents and climate in the North Atlantic.

Climate and volcanism have had a major impact on the fortunes of the Icelandic nation over the centuries. But changes caused by the activities of man himself might prove to be the most decisive of all for the fate of the weather and natural conditions in Iceland in the future.

Hljómskálagarðurinn Park and the Lake in Reykjavík.
The first community began to develop in the dip in the land north of the Lake in the
mid-18th century, and the oldest houses in the capital date from that time.

Many statues and sculptures adorn Reykjavík, even though it is a young city.
Ásmundur Sveinsson (1893-1982) made the Water Carrier in 1936.
In the background is the Pearl, on top of Reykjavík Energy's geothermal
water distribution tanks on Öskjuhlíð hill.

Reykjavík is renowned for its lively nightlife, with numerous nightclubs,
pubs and discotheques large and small.
The photo is taken in the ballroom of Broadway at Hótel Ísland.

A sunny summer's day on Austurvöllur in Reykjavík city centre.
The pavement café recalls more southerly latitudes.

Parliament House on Austurvöllur was built in 1880-81. Iceland's parliament
has met there ever since, but it also housed various other activities at first.
The University of Iceland had facilities there for almost 30 years after its establishment in 1911.

The pavilion which gives Hljómskálagarðurinn ("Pavilion Garden") its name, seen from across the Lake.
Built in 1922-23 by the Reykjavík Brass Band, the pavilion was the first building in Iceland exclusively dedicated to music.

Firework displays can be spectacular in the twilight of summer, not just in darkness.
The night sky bursts into colour during celebrations to mark Reykjavík's "Harbour Days."

In the interior of Borgarfjörður, Hvítá river flows along the edge of Hallmundarhraun lava field.
This young lava is porous and water which permeates it eventually enters Hvítá in a broad waterfall, Hraunfossar.

Barnafoss waterfall on Hvítá river, just above Hraunfossar in Borgarfjörður.
A stone arch crosses the fall where the river narrows.
The name Barnafoss ("Children's Waterfall") derives from two children said
to have drowned after falling from an earlier natural bridge.

Caves are sometimes created in lava when magma flows beneath the congealed surface, often for long distances.
A cave is then left when the eruption stops.
The photo is from Raufarhólshellir, where icicles glitter in the candlelight.

A few lava flows have formed in eruptions in West Iceland since the end of the Ice Age 10,000 years ago. One eruption several thousand years ago created the exceptionally symmetrical lava ring Eldborg.

Rauðfeldargjá gully on Snæfellsnes peninsula, which cuts down through the foot of Mt. Botnsfjall.
The gully is named after Rauðfeldur Þorkelsson,
whom the hero of the Saga of Bárður Snæfellsás is said to have thrown into it.

The majestic Snæfellsjökull glacier (1446 m) stands out on the end of Snæfellsnes peninsula.
Few experiences are more magical than standing on the top of Snæfellsjökull in the midnight sun,
watching the sea that surrounds it on three sides.

Flatey, one of the largest of the numerous islands in Breiðafjörður Bay, was a trading post for centuries
and an important cultural centre in the 19th century.
Advances in transport, fishing methods and technology in the 20th century have caused
the Breiðafjörður islands to become depopulated, and Flatey is no exception.
Today, it is mainly inhabited in summer only.

The shore of Rauðisandur.
Sand in Iceland is generally formed from rock fragments,
and the predominance of basaltic rocks means that most sand is black.
In some places, however, are sandshell beaches, which are light brown.

Þingeyri in Dýrafjörður, with the mountains separating it from Arnarfjörður in the background.
One of Iceland's many villages which have been built up around fishing and fish processing,
Þingeyri began to develop towards the end of the 19th century.

Formed by the erosion of Ice Age glaciers and fenced in by steep mountains on both sides,
Önundarfjörður is in many ways typical of the West Fjords (Vestfirðir).
In transversal valleys and at the head of the fjord people have lived for centuries, earning their
livelihoods from the sea and from farming.

Hornstrandir turns a luxurious green in summer and an astonishing amount of
vegetation covers the massive bird cliffs, fertilized by bird droppings.
View to the east from Hvannadalur across to the peaks of Miðfell, Jörundur
and Kálfatindar on Hornbjarg.

Puffins on the Látrabjarg cliffs.
Thought to be the most common bird in Iceland, the puffin is found all around the coast.

The northernmost region of the West Fjords is Hornstrandir.
Hornbjarg cliff rises from the fog in the evening light.
Hornstrandir is the closest part of Iceland to Greenland
and sea ice sometimes drifts down from there in late winter.

Hornvík, west of Hornbjarg, is a fertile bay and a popular spot with summer travellers.
It can only be reached on foot or by boat. Once quite populated, Hornstrandir has been uninhabited for several decades.

From Gjögur on Strandir. In the background the mountains of Reykjafjörður and Veiðileysufjörður rise steeply from the sea. Farthest to the left is Birgisvíkurfjall. In earlier times there was much fishing from Gjögur, including fishing for shark, but this discontinued some time ago.

Akureyri, the main town of north Iceland (pop. 15,000).
Its sheltered location at the head of Eyjafjörður fjord means the weather
is much better than in most other parts of the north.
Akureyri has strong manufacturing and fishing industries, as well as museums, an art college,
a rapidly growing university and its own professional theatre company.

LAND OF LIGHT

Mt. Hverfjall by Lake Mývatn is an ash ring, a crater
formed in a huge ash eruption 2,500 years ago.
The crater measures 1,200 m in diameter and the walls
tower 150 m above their surroundings.
Hverfjall is one of the largest known ash rings on Earth.

Winter at Kálfastrandarvogar by Lake Mývatn.
Its wealth of lava formations include the Klasar rock stacks which stand up from the water.

Although Mývatn is at a highland elevation, it has been home
to a flourishing community for centuries. View from Kálfastrandarvogar.

Few places can match Mývatn for the diversity of its lava formations.
At Dimmuborgir, part of the lava flood flowed away while the rest congealed
into bizarre crags and natural sculptures.

The most majestic waterfall series in Iceland is where the river Jökulsá á Fjöllum
enters Jökulsárgljúfur canyon, which was formed by a catastrophic
glacier outburst flood several thousands of years ago.
Dettifoss, photographed here, is the greatest of the Jökulsá waterfalls.

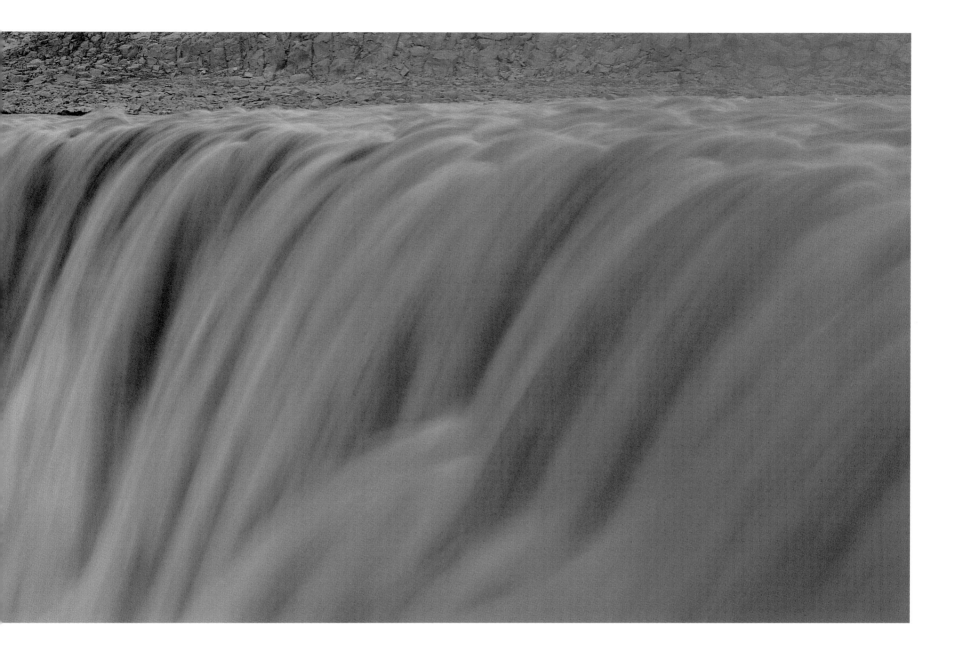

Iceland is a showcase of the contrasting forces of ice and fire.
Vatnajökull is by far the largest of the several glaciers in the highlands.
Kverkfjöll on its northern rim is one of the most powerful geothermal fields in Iceland.
It is partly submerged under the glacier, and the geothermal heat melts caves and holes into the ice.

Fumarole at Kverkfjöll.
Geothermal heat transforms the rock and tints it light brown.
Kverkfjöll is a large volcanic centre but no verified eruptions have taken place there in historical times.

Víti ("Hell") in the Askja caldera where the water is at a comfortable temperature for bathing and a popular attraction for travellers.
Víti is an explosion crater formed at the end of the massive eruption in Askja in 1875.
Fallout of ash from the eruption caused great hardship to farmers in East Iceland and partly prompted
the widespread emigration from that region to America.

Sometimes called "the queen of Icelandic mountains," Herðubreið is a classic table mountain.
These were formed in subglacial eruptions during the Ice Age.
It is estimated that Herðubreið was formed when the glacier was at least 1,000 m thick.

LAND OF LIGHT

Eyjabakkar and Snæfell, a marshy area with numerous ponds and lagoons.
The river Jökulsá á Fljótsdal meanders through the area from
its source in Eyjabakkajökull.
Eyjabakkar is an important refuge for vast numbers of pink-footed
geese in summer, when they are moulting.
Very shy and easily frightened, they often form large groups out
on the water.

Autumn at Eskifjörður.
As in West Iceland, the mountains are sheer and formed from regular walls of cliffs with grassy escarpments.
The cliffs are ancient lava that flowed around 10 million years ago.

Dyrfjöll mountains in Borgarfjörður eystri, East Iceland.
An Ice Age glacier was the main force shaping these mountains, carving
and etching them into sharp peaks and sheer cliff faces.

Breiðdalur.
Most of the strata in East Iceland have a western inclination, towards the land.
The mountains in the photograph are relics of an old, extinct volcanic centre which was active millions of years ago.

Lónsöræfi on the eastern rim of Vatnajökull is a paradise for hikers.
Tröllakrókar is a bizarre creation where water and wind have combined to conjure up a feast for the traveller's eye.

View to the south across Papafjörður in Lón on a bright autumn day.
Brunnhorn and Vestrahorn, the two mountains, are formed from plutonic rock
which has congealed deep below the earth's surface.

Reindeer are one of the few species of wild mammal in Iceland and are found in the wilderness of the east.
Their history in Iceland only extends back 200 years – they were first imported from Norway in 1771.
The stock now numbers 2-3,000 animals.

In autumn 1996 a sizeable eruption took place at the volcano Gjálp in Vatnajökull, north of Grímsvötn.
A huge amount of ice was melted and burst forth on November 5, 1996, flooding the entire Skeiðarársandur
area and causing heavy damage to roads and bridges.
The outburst tore fragments from the glacier and swept large icebergs down the course of the river.

Kálfafellsdalur valley inland from Suðursveit, walled in on either side by dramatic mountains.
The landscape is more Alpine in character than in most other parts of Iceland. Brókarjökull glacier descends
into the head of the valley and Steinavötn flows down from it. In earlier times, Brókarjökull extended farther along
the valley, blocking another valley, Vatnsdalur, which transects it.
Occasional glacier outburst floods occurred when amassed water burst from Vatnsdalur.

Skálafellsjökull glacier on the southeastern rim of Vatnajökull.
Sharp peaks and crests delimit the edge of the highlands.
The expanses of the glacier stretch northwards, while sheer cliffs and steep mountainsides lie to the south.
Skálafellsjökull is the centre for snowscooter expeditions on Vatnajökull.

Jökulsárlón glacier lagoon.
Icebergs calve into the lagoon from the snout of Breiðamerkurjökull glacier which creeps out into it.
The lagoon has been formed over the past 60 years, as the glacier retreats with the warming in the climate.

Bright evening at Jökulsárlón lagoon.
Icebergs calve from the glacier and float in the lagoon until they run aground where the river Jökulsá drains from it.

Ice cave under Breiðamerkurjökull glacier.
Water runs through tunnels at the bottom of the glacier near its snout.
If the river course shifts, the tunnel collapses.
A preserved subglacial tunnel which can be entered is a rare sight – but this photo was
taken inside one, on a course that the river Breiðá abandoned beneath Breiðamerkurjökull.
The tunnel collapsed and vanished within the space of a few months.

Bales of hay collected from a meadow in Öræfasveit.
Haymaking was one of many aspects of farming that were revolutionized by mechanization.
For centuries, hay was cut using scythes, which was a slow and laborious job.

Man and nature live in exceptionally close contact in Öræfasveit.
The farm Skaftafell (left) stands only 3 km from the snout of Skaftafellsjökull glacier.

Eruption in Grímsvötn, December 1998.
Beneath Vatnajökull glacier is Iceland's most active volcanic area.
Activity centres on Grímsvötn, which has erupted more often in
historical times than any other volcano in Iceland.
Grímsvötn is also the source of regular glacial outburst floods, some
of which have swamped the Skeiðarársandur sands, although in recent
decades most of them have been less dramatic.

Arctic riverbeauty flowers in early summer on moist sands.
It adds a rare dash of living colour to otherwise barren sands,
especially in the highlands.
The photograph was taken on the western edge of Skeiðarársandur,
by the Núpsvatn bridge, with Mt. Lómagnúpur in the background.

Núpsstaður nestles beneath the western slopes of Lómagnúpur and is the easternmost farm in Fljótshverfi district. Local farmers often guided travellers on horseback over the unbridged rivers on Skeiðarársandur in the old days. The turfbuilt chapel at Núpsstaður is one of the oldest buildings preserved in Iceland, dating from the 17th century.

One of the many craters in the 27 km Lakagígar series.
Lava flowed from the crater through the breach in its wall.

Námshraun lava field flowed from a crater in the saddle between the Norðurnámur
and Suðurnámur mountains in the same eruption that created
Laugahraun and the Veiðivötn lakes around 1480.
Lake Frostastaðavatn in the foreground.

Highland soil erosion and desertification are one of the more serious environmental problems that Iceland faces.
From the highlands north of Mýrdalsjökull ice cap.

North Emstruá river. Most of the Icelandic highlands are barren with scant vegetation, characterized by lava fields and sands. Here the river has formed a shallow chasm with the lava clearly visible on its wall.

The wetlands of Blautulón north of Eldgjá.
The highlands abound in sharp contrasts. In the area between the Tungnaá and Skaftá rivers,
the typical landscape is hyaloclastite ridges separated by occasional perfectly flat plains,
sometimes covered with moss where there is ample moisture.

Landmannalaugar.
Rich red hues of rhyolite dominate in the surrounding mountains, which belong to the powerful volcanic centre
in the Torfajökull area. These rhyolite mountains were formed by eruptions beneath the Ice Age glacier, while
the lava by the springs was created just over 500 years ago, during the eruption that created the Veiðivötn lake system.

Geothermal activity at Brennisteinsalda close to Landmannalaugar.
The area around Landmannalaugar, within the Torfajökull volcanic centre,
is one of the most intense geothermal fields in Iceland.

Landmannalaugar is one of Iceland's most popular spots for travellers,
and the hot pools after which it is named are one of its main attractions.

Sharply contrasting colours around Landmannalaugar.
In the foreground is moss-covered lava where Jökulgilskvísl flows over light rhyolite flats.
Rich green moss covers the slopes in the background, capped by the brown and barren
mountain with patches of last winter's snows.

Near Landmannalaugar.
Glaciers and water have been the primary agents shaping the hyaloclastite and rhyolite areas of the highlands.
Most of the mountains were formed by subglacial eruptions, then chiselled and hewn by glaciers.
After the glacier cover lifted, water has carved out gullies and creeks.

Tungnaá and Svartikrókur, with the Torfajökull area in the distance.
Although Tungnaá's source is the Vatnajökull ice cap it meanders slowly at Svartikrókur, which
was once a lagoon where the river deposited its sediment.

A variety of materials are deposited by hot springs, often forming coatings of silicon and sulphur.
Species of thermophilic (heat-loving) algae and bacteria which thrive in such hot springs
are being eagerly studied by scientists.

The delicate green hue of fountain apple moss is a delightful sight.
This moss, shown here at Hungursfit north of Tindfjallajökull, grows where there
is adequate moisture, often in sandy terrain.

Afternoon light over the Veiðivötn lakes.
Powerful volcanic eruptions have taken place in the area since the settlement of Iceland. In the distance
is Vatnaöldur, a crater row formed just before 900 in the eruption which deposited "the settlement layer" of ash
over most of Iceland, now used for geological and archaeological dating.
The lakes themselves are in part explosion craters from a massive eruption around 1480.

View of the 1991 Hekla eruption from the town of Hella, with the tranquil
river Ytri-Rangá in the foreground. Some Hekla eruptions have melted ice on the slopes of the volcano
to produce flood bursts in Ytri-Rangá, although this was not the case in 1991.

Mt. Hekla.
Together with Katla and Grímsvötn, Hekla is one of the most active volcanoes in Iceland, erupting on at least 17 known occasions since the settlement. Several eruptions have taken place in the vicinity of Hekla too, including one in 1554 in Vondubjallar, the craters in the foreground.

Gígjökull creeps down from Eyjafjallajökull onto the lowlands.
Like other glaciers, Gígjökull has retreated noticeably in the 20th century.
Until just before 1930 the snout of the glacier was at the site of the present bridge.
The glacier is a popular training ground for climbers.

Þórsmörk's diverse landscape is shaped by water and glaciers which have eroded the hyaloclastite rock.
It spans the spectrum from woodlands with sheltered camping spots to colourful bird life and beautiful views of glaciers.
Húsadalur valley in the foreground and the ice-covered Eyjafjallajökull volcano in the background.

View eastwards to Mýrdalsjökull across the Krossá river flats in Þórsmörk.
Þórsmörk is a popular destination for travellers, even though the road there crosses several
unbridged rivers and is only accessible by large 4WD vehicles.

People go to Þórsmörk at all times of year, to delight in
seeing its many faces. New Year's Eve celebrations at Básar,
with a bonfire and northern lights.

Þjórsá (shown here) and Ölfusá are the rivers with the highest rate of flow in Iceland.
Four separate glaciers – Vatnajökull, Hofsjökull, Tungnafellsjökull and Torfajökull – drain into Þjórsá.
A number of hydropower plants have been built on Þjórsá and its tributary,
Tungnaá, and form the backbone of Iceland's electricity system.

Skarðshlíð and Hrútafell, at the foot of Eyjafjöll. In the background are
Raufarfell and the Kaldaklifsjökull snout from Eyjafjallajökull.
Eyjafjöll and Mýrdalur are the southernmost parts of Iceland's mainland, where spring
generally arrives first in Iceland and the land is grassy and fertile.

Gullfoss waterfall on the river Hvítá, a spectacular display of unharnessed natural energy.
One of the pioneers in nature conservation in Iceland was Sigríður Tómasdóttir from Brattholt, who early this century
campaigned against Gullfoss being controlled by a private company which planned to harness it for hydropower.
After years of campaigning Gullfoss became the property of the Icelandic state and today most people would think
it absurd to sacrifice "the Golden Waterfall" in order to generate electricity.

A number of geysers are found in Iceland.
The most famous of all, Geysir in Haukadalur, even gave its name to this phenomenon.
Geysir only spouts rarely these days, but nearby Strokkur (shown here) is very active.

Geothermal and volcanic activity are closely linked phenomena.
The most powerful geothermal fields are in or near to active volcanic centres, such as
these springs near Hrafntinnusker by Torfajökull.
The geothermal activity there is explained by cooling of warm rock in the roots of the volcanic centre.

Relentless surf from North Atlantic rollers pounds the shores of south Iceland.
Several mountains and bluffs extend to the shore in Mýrdalur, including Dyrhólaey (shown here).
It is made of hyaloclastite, the product of a submarine eruption, and boats can sail through the hole,
which measures several tens of metres high.

Late winter on Mt. Skjaldbreið.
Winter travel is very popular among owners of jeeps and trucks who have developed
a technique for driving over the snow-covered highlands.
Jeeps are fitted with huge reinforced tyres from which almost all the air pressure is removed, to make
the vehicle "float" on the snow. In good weather, there's hardly any obstacle to driving anywhere in the wilds.

Small waterfalls in Gjáin in Þjórsárdalur valley donning their winter garb.
Some falls disappear completely in winter beneath a hard cover of ice.

From Þingvellir, with Lake Þingvallavatn in the distance. The site of Iceland's parliament from 930 to 1798, Þingvellir is now a National Park. The plains are in a rift valley between Almannagjá and Hrafnagjá. The picture shows the sheer western wall of Almannagjá and the slope down into the valley. Þingvellir sank by almost one metre in an earthquake in 1789.

The Blue Lagoon at Svartsengi, one of the most popular attractions among travellers to Iceland.
It is formed by runoff geothermal water from the Suðurnes District Heating Utility power station.

Leifur Eiríksson terminal at Keflavík Airport is the first glimpse which most visitors to Iceland have of the country.
The terminal is named after Leif the Lucky, discoverer of America in the year 1000.
In the foreground is the sculpture Jet Nest by Magnús Tómasson.

Winter atmosphere in downtown Reykjavík.

Cafés have grown and flourished in Reykjavík in recent years, particularly in the city centre.

Hamlet by William Shakespeare at the National Theatre of Iceland, 1997.
Hilmir Snær Guðnason (Hamlet) and Ingvar E. Sigurðsson (Claudius).
Design: Vytautas Narbutas. Director: Baltasar Kormákur.

Winter weather is always changeable in Iceland, and Reykjavík is no exception.
But sometimes this can mean a change for the better, and it's fun to stroll the streets on a calm and sunny winter's day.
Scene from Fríkirkjuvegur with the Lutheran Free Church in the background.

Northern lights above Reykjavík.
Produced by the interaction of solar winds and the magnetic field of the Earth, northern lights
(aurora borealis) are only visible close to the North and South Poles, where the magnetic
lines of force concentrate and approach the surface of the Earth.

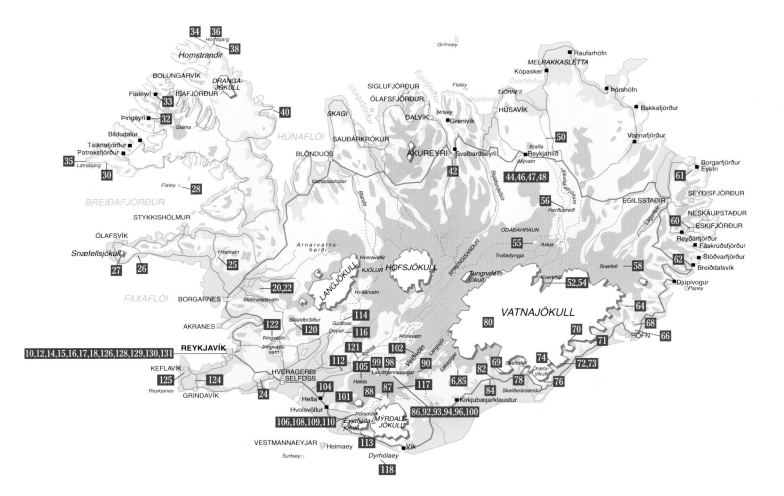

LAND OF LIGHT

Foreword · Ólafur Ragnar Grímsson, President of Iceland

Photographs · Haukur Snorrason, photographer
Texts · Magnús Tumi Guðmundsson, geophysicist
Design · Ólöf Jóna Guðmundsdóttir, graphic artist
Production · Snorri Snorrason, editor/publisher
Selection of photographs and print supervision · Haukur Snorrason and Snorri Snorrason
English translation and proofreading · Bernard Scudder for Orðabankinn sf.
Local maps · Guðmundur Ó Ingvarsson, geographer
Map of Iceland · Iceland Geodetic Survey
Photographs of the Water Carrier by Ásmundur Sveinsson and Jet Nest by Magnús Tómasson
are printed with the permission of Myndstef, the Icelandic Visual Arts Copyright Association
Cameras · Pentax 6x7 · Fuji G 617 Panorama · Nikon FM2 · Hasselblad 500 C/M
Films: Fujichrome Velvia · Kodak 100 SW
Film developing · Egill ljósmyndaþjónusta · Skyggna Myndverk
Typesetting · layout · colour separations · printing · binding · Oddi hf.
Publisher · SNERRUÚTGÁFAN ehf · PO Box 12210 · 132 Reykjavík · Iceland
Fax (+354) 567 6671 · e-mail · snerra@simnet.is · www.simnet.is/snerra

ISBN 9979-9238-2-2
21702
© 1999/2000 Snerruútgáfan ehf.